MILES PRESS

Indiana University South Bend Department of English

THE

BOTTOM

42 Miles Press
Editor, David Dodd Lee
Copyright© 2014 Betsy Andrews. All rights reserved.
ISBN 978-0-9830747-5-5 (pbk. alk. paper)

For permission, required to reprint or broadcast more than several lines, write to:
42 Miles Press, Department of English, Indiana University South Bend
1700 Mishawaka Avenue, South Bend, IN 46615

http://42milespress.com

Art Direction, Nick Kuder, Design, Ashley Orban, Production, Paul Sizer
The Design Center, Frostic School Of Art, Western Michigan University.
Printing, McNaughton & Gunn, Inc.

THE
BOTTOM

A
POEM
BY
BETSY
ANDREWS

Nay, tiny shell-bird,
What a huge vast inanimate it is, that you must row against,
What an incalculable inertia.

– D.H. Lawrence, *Baby Tortoise*

CONTENTS

THE BOTTOM

Atop the bottom, the water-ghost
the riddle-ghost tower, fireballs lapping the ghost map
the ghost nets, the ghost moon, the ghost lines, the ghost traps,
the fingerlings giving up ghost
the long dark drive, the ghost drive, over the derelict moat
the ghost era's ghost-dish, its secrets, its swallows,
its test site's thousand ghost bites named for rivers
and ice caps and nautical terms, for fish and for towns named for ghost
the long-gone ghost of the beaver meadow, *Las Vegas* they called it, skinned
ghost wagers streaming in
the once-and-again wealth of the nation a tour-tram parking lot coast
ghost of the barnacled schoolroom, lesson a nibbling ghost
In the hook-and-sink daybreak
at the ghost-black terminal, its scaffolds and catwalks and ladders and berths,
gunships its ghost-and-ghost host,
a borne-again freighter named *Universal Hope* is suckling, is guzzling up the ghost
in the cold commons' ghost mouth, a trio of pearls,
three itches enraptured by ghost
the narwhal the sea cow the sea mink the monk seal a mouthful of ghost word, extinct
the half-seas' coral a ghost story written in bone-white ink
The king counts his ghostlands,
his wrecks and his flotsam, his jetsam, his water-strays, his fishes.
My wish is: We are on the shore, we are looking out at the water.
You are lying beside me, curled.
The sun is coming up. I am turning you over
I am going to see your face
The sun is coming up, I am turning you over
I am going to be able to see your face

the morning is a vexing, it is chamber-sweep and quarrel,
quickening fruit for the water-thieves, vacationers mugging the coral
the morning is a shell-drift, an addle-egg, a purse
bursting with subsidized removals; a welter heap, an ash pot, a curse
upon the harbor, its beige-on-beige huskings, its loss;
as a matter of public policy, it's a stink-broth bewitched at the cost
of the fledglings, the hatchlings, the sanderlings, the crabs
the morning is shelter-throat, it's shake-foot and scabs
from a night wheeling 10,000 valves beneath the streets
while the numbed city slumbers atop its thirst-keep
the morning is a taking, it's a 60-mile plunder,
sweet spot for the dead-zone cats clawing holes down under
the morning is a double-down on the secrets at the bottom,
it is by-kill, it is *has-to-be*, it is industry, it's a sodden
living for "the living," by which we mean Man
the morning is a vexing; it is catch as catch can

the women who follow the herring shoals
the women who walk the coast
at eightpence an hour, the harbor host
to a thousand smacks of the oceans' envy—
the dogfish, the cachalot, the thresher, the minke
bitten by a dog on a mile-long chain,
the huers spelling again and again
the end of another vicious enrapture—
roll fingers in sacks vacant of flour
take knives to the belly of that they call "darling"
it's a job; and the word, grown up from the skerries and docks,
speaks leagues of our need to clock taking in order to live
darling, the bottom is thoroughly touched
it is tractored and train-tracked and floodlit with grid,
the remains of a scuttled crab pot,
its lid long since tossed to the porpoise-show public,
where the Prince of Humbugs counts his receipts,
hammering Jumbo with rotgut
"There was Mystery," the Mock Turtle sighs,
"There was Drawling, Stretching, and Fainting in Coils"
until the water froze in the firemen's hose,
the seals flopping out on the downtown cobble,
the whales boiled in their tanks—it stank for days of dead giant
it's pliant, the bottom, it can be caned and rushed
and scraped from the cask and shorn from the wig
and tilled and tooled and authored
but its blackblues are the blackblues of nowhere on surface
and we have better relations with Mars

this is a diary of my molting, love, a drawer with a false bottom fathomed
in so many feathers, it could be a kill; this is a gang of knives at the hinges,
a fistful's syringes, the oyster doped up for a truth; this is a shell game disrobed
on this bone-gone globe, scrapings from the backsides of boots to deduce
how we can stand ourselves, where we are coming from, which is
Devil's Hole where the few stray pupfish park, which is
Devil's Den emptied of its bitters and larks, which is
Devil's Point where the sea bats are yanked from the sea; which is a submarine called
Devilfish, where the devil's tongue licks the ribs of the pollywogs and
the right whales and the killer whales and dolphins, hot-forked and branded
and stranded in the gloom, the 200-decibel mid-frequency boom shaking them
apart at the seams; in dreams I see pilings that even shipworms have forsaken,
it has taken 19 tons of cruise ship gunk to debunk this billion-dollar beachfront shanty:
By the sea, by the sea, by the beautiful sea, you and I, you and I, oh how happy we'll be
no matter the sixtieth seconds we take, it's just not the case that a tick-tock of sand
was all that spaced the Jamestown colonists from the "happy shores of the Pacific";
the terrific ephemera of the nepe tide our bedding—the fish floats and hazard drums
and barnacled skiffs, the polypropylene doodads and the netting adrift and face-blind—
we find ourselves nevertheless, two closely spanned, soft-bodied curves,
a best guess at the theory of elasticity

a jellyfish hitches a ride on a gallon jug called Tide

finds itself in an unfamiliar ocean, the notion of national sovereignty

upended by thermal convection; behind the high-voltage barricade beside the sylvan shore

where Camp Delta takes to its Coppertone, the clean team is doing its chore,

sweeping a Supermax cage. "We'll show him a map," says Admiral Task Force,

raising his one-star flag. "Then it's, 'Thanks a lot. Have a Big Mac.'"

Another fine day for Air Sunshine, offshore duty heating up, cruisewear on sale at the PX,

the stock clerk's cup of coffee 140 liters past due on the Aral Sea,

the Yangtze, the Indus, the Nile, the Ravi, the Niger, the Congo, the Volta, the Volga;

the Orange, Yellow, Blue, and Black Rivers, the Blue and Green Lakes,

the rivers named Crocodile and Snake be damned for the license to Have It Your Way

the jellyfish, in the meantime, has administered a sting—it's a jellyfish thing;

it's eating, it's spring-load survival;

the Bible the model for scourges, the government urges the parting of seas,

the burning of dune grass, the slaughter of the jellyfish first-born

it's like porn, it's a snuff film called *Pest*; out west, Fish and Wildlife plays Ahab to

the prodigious northern pike, its paper-and-spit lookalike burned in effigy

by a citzenry parched by the cure, their taps gone impure with the pesticide drip,

a 17,000-gallon fouled sip to fatten the goose of the

Chem-Fish, Fish Nox, Noxfire, Tox-R door-to-door salesmen

a whelk attaches itself to a turbine,
gets the lift of its life at the world's first-ever wave farm
"It's an industry waiting to happen," says the analyst, minus one discombobulated snail,
the pail of water that Jack and Jill fetched a tumble worth 400 billion clams
"Of course we're investing significantly in water," says the chemical company executive,
how a feckless approach to an everyday thirst can tap a blistering business,
an entrepreneurial urgency to fill oil tankers with drool; stockholders half-seas over,
black teeth awash, screwed to the eyeballs, pissed and sloshed and sozzled on the stuff
that falls in vaults and catacombs; Henry Hudson, cruising the gnomes,
makes off with a jug of their whiskey, a frisky brew stewed from the juices of the river
he christened "Gimmee"; his crew, turned to pygmies, mutinies and strands him on a rock;
it's a PR conundrum, the gut-level aversion most people have to a glassful of swill
still, every time the water portfolio manager flushes his toilet, it rains

"I've been very mindful of the appearance of conflict and operated accordingly,"
says the Interior Department's new hack, meaning
he keeps that leftover freeholders' check hidden behind his back
when he ladles federal bloat in their bowls that they spoon to Los Angeles for profit
the Central Valley Project a water fowl stuffed with arcane writ,
a 50-year infusion for the almonds' IV drip
a view of conflict obstructed by a no-swim sign at the aqueduct;
appearances being what they are, we're far too far from the floating object
not to insist on land-ho, Captain Cook boiling over with the "pleasure of being first,"
though he appears to have been a run-of-the-mill dish on the Islands of Sandwich;
what appears to be dead fish in the Tigris are Baghdad's Hun-flung books;
what appears to be dead fish in the Klamath River are dead fish, hooked
by a vice-presidential angler, the Endangered Species Act a catch
rotting from head to bladder, baited with mid-term agri-votes
the moat around the White House a drowning hazard for government-fed biologists

800 brands of barbed wire swaddle a lockbox at the Slippery Bank,
a bottom fisher's biofuel, an orangutan ransomed for lip gloss,
the starving of birds for an industry standard on the measure of pathos in love songs,
the ad man's lunch a powder puff flattened by radial tires,
Dear Leader's need for comfy dreams a knock on the chin of a million sparrows
"I don't want to spoil anyone's fun," the resort community ecologist says,
"but I'm trying to save an endangered species."
a fireworks of celebrity recipes for making oneself feel hot,
based on the common misconception that megalomania tastes like chicken,
the boom in nude disaster tours, a storefront sale on putrefaction,
an aquarium rendered a barracks, an aquarium rendered a morgue;
when the needles refuse their turn on the astrolabe factory picket line,
the Worshipful Company of Clockmakers, infested with feverish ticks,
proposes a means of navigating by the yelp of wounded dogs because
sympathy proves the correctness of the mariner's moral compass,
another protest for the plight of the penguins mounted by hitting "send"

to get to the bottom of this fishy deal, we'll have to walk the plank
sink us down with a long, long roll
where the sharks'll have our bodies, and the devil have our souls
with the hagfish and snot worms and cutthroat eels,
we'll pull bottom-wool off sailors' bones to make our sodden meals
oh, a mermaid's life is full of strife with men of ease or business
from our heads to our waist, we're just their taste but after that, we're fishes
1830: Farmers cutting seaweed to spread on their potato fields spy a creature thrashing
in the water. A boy hits her on the head with a rock, and she dies. Washed ashore, she is
the length of a four-year-old with an outsized chest and a lower half that looks like a salmon
without scales. The factor of Benbecula orders a coffin and buries her on the shores of Culla Bay.
1717: Dutch sailors catch a creature off the coast of Borneo. She cries the cries of a little mouse
and shits the shit of kittens. They keep her in a barrel for four days and seven hours, and she
dies. The Czar of Russia, Peter the Great, is so moved by a picture of the creature in a book that
he travels in disguise across Europe to Amsterdam to press the publisher for further proof.
1620: Charged with securing a colony for the venture capitalist Sir William Vaughn, Captain
Richard Whitbourne sails to New-found-land where a beauteous creature with hair of blue
swims up to his boat. A crewman smacks her head with an oar, and she sinks into the sea.
at the bottom of the sea, a whale fall feeds a world—
mucous eels and giant clams and sleeper sharks and you and me
if we sink in that lonely, lonesome water, if we sink into that lonesome sea

Mr. Limpet, minding his business, swept up in the trawl of the dawn's early light
with the yellowtail, the cod, the haddock, the flounder, the halibut, the butterfish,
the dogfish, the glass squid, the Yeti crab, basket star, deep-sea dancer,
the Gorgon's head, the armored sea robin, the sea angel, seadevil, sea pig, the squirt,
the glowing sea cucumber, the small croaking sculpin, the orange sponge called monkey dung,
the gulper eel, dragonfish, black-belly sucker, the red paper lantern, the heart urchin,
fangtooth, the spookfish, the blacksnout, the kelp, the stones, the porpoise bones;
then the trawls trawl trawls, they trawl and trawl trawls until the trawls are all they're trawling,
a special on trawl at Maison de La Mer, *Fillet du Trawl Marinière*;
Mr. Limpet, his twilight last gleaming, disembarks in a crateful of ice

morning is a half-baked bird, a water-poet's nonsense, a newscast hulled like coconuts,
a swindle in the cartographic conscience—how half a hundred atlas makers
stroke the climes and bow the lakes and twang the vegetation
but neglect to thrum the dented drum of the grubbed and rubbled mountain,
where a list of furry woodland critters subject to evacuation
on a signpost by the impoundment ditch serves as "habitat reclamation"
at the overburdened gash that keeps the lights on in distant states,
the Appalachian faucets running orange;
at the far end of this page, there's a wood rat who loves pretty things
he's scrounging in our flyrock for shotgun shells and shards of glass to carry to his burrow
in the center, there's a fleet of D-9 dozers chewing furrows in the skyline
where the mountain used to be; and the sea?
it's in the margins here—its teeny-tiny winglike fins folded in

to sound like itself is what water wants, to look like itself, to feel wet
walloped by cinderblock, spars and bottles, the wanting-locked water lay down
the wanting-locked water lay down its lustre, it lay down its lustre and stank
the wanting-locked water stank without lustre, it stank without lustre and we
cut it with knives; we cut it with scissors, the wanting-locked water, we cut it
with radars, we ginned it; the wanting-locked water was ginned and engined,
we engined and cinch-lipped and quicksilvered water; the water was baited
with nixies and bogles, it was looted of moon, it was piss-and-spit crooked;
the water engaged in protective reactions—it limped, it wore bright orange pants
the wanting-locked water was orange with panting, it was orange and panting,
it stank. "I want a clean cup," interrupted the Hatter: "let's all move one place on."
One place on, the octopus burrowed into a crevice of the Duotex blow-up boat,
by the recessed valve between the self-bailing floor and the thermobonded
bouyancy tube, the octopus burrowed, slender and orange, the wonderpus
burrowed, thinking, "this is coral, it's rock crack, it's shell"; its slot-box eyes
clanging like bells on hillocks, its ginger arms stroking; the sun beat down, the
stories were told of the last of the last of the last Martian race,
with bodies like mazes and three beating hearts; the day went on day,
the sun turned away, the octopus turned a Duotex grey, and, finally,
from the captain's fingers it slipped, dipping its quill in its damning pot and
scribbling rage at the lot of us on the illuminated page of the ocean, fuck you
in the name of the tide pools and shrimp haunts; to eat is what the octopus wants,
its excitable beak, its gifted locomotion, what the octopus wants is to live

you want blue, my love, you want black;
you want that for which teeth approach flesh, the "factual"
in the broken rondel of the fresh-cracked shell, a gulping that signals a throat;
a pack of spades, the die's beady eye, the midwater's shivering timbers
tucked in the bolt-upright lap of the drowned, as mum as birds in a wiretapped nest,
a choke-damp scam on the black-bagged sand, the waves juiced like sour cherries;
you want liquor that skins the grammar from tongues and
lock-picks the breath like a twist-off cap;
I can pantomime the sea at a loitering boil; I can draw a map knotted with sea snakes,
but you want world topside down, you want teets and hackles;
you want the compression of stars, my love,
those billion-ton hangers-on of the heavens, the mariner's Black Jack jars;
I give you lap-pool blackout, I give you shark in a box

the channel is a working-class stiff: bouys and ragged Confederate flags,
a coveline of crosses on cliffs; "Look what they built us," the pelicans think,
concrete piers and signal towers, all good things to shit on;
the pelicans sit on the dock and take stock: behind the fish, a fish, they say,
and behind that fish, no fish at all, and behind no fish, no fishes;
it's a port full of spines and postcard designs on the bite left behind in the sea wrack,
a Kodak stab at a shame-faced crab, a can-opener rescue for the chowder shack;
from here, the pelting and the smelting are emptied into the harbor
further out, roustabouts, roughnecks and derrick hands get paid to raid the larder;
in the bed below the ferryboats, the cars on board umbilical, all of us driving farther
away from the steeplejack sea in a race to be drier than drenched;
from the jackup rigs and the tension-leg benches a blaze like St. Elmo's fire,
a sound like the sound of a voice, it's multiple choice on the subject of "bleak" versus "dire"
"Science is inquiry, not answers," says the chemist sipping the pot-boiler Gulf;
from atop the continental shelf, Humpty Dumpty's daredevil fall,
the bore that bores at the yolk of it all, a dredging as thorough as Darwin
"I can't go no lower," said the Hatter: "I'm on the floor, as it is."

a little lonely ship to shore; say pelican, think regret

dynamite fouls a pelican's jowls,

and what're you gonna do about it, stumblebum?

sorrow dog, landlocked, sits on the rug; I've shipped out to industry's ocean

happy dog beats her tail on the floor; I'm home once more

with a rucksack of nudge and commotion

oh, sorrow dog, the loblolly boys and their sick-bay gruel

almost fooled us with bunkum forevers;

but cure-alls won't quarrel with a febrile bitch

and swallows don't nap in the ice-cold sea

and night scrapes at night like a dash-throat razor

her lungs, catching up to her heart, exhaled, her skin her fur, her fur

and me? a little lonely now shore to ship, pox and rot and flux and itch

the mermaids raise their hands; they would like to ask a question
they are unfamiliar with microphones, and the flotational devices of the press pool
but they recognize a wave when they see one—
they can mimic the speed of sound in air;
when called on, the mermaids manage their mouths into the shape of "What is that?"
it's a riddle twice as inflated as Texas; it's six times the weight of the plankton seas
it's a teaser rendered in styrene with the acronym PCB
it's albatross innards decoded as omen; it's a starfish-crossed plea
it's a whopper, and the flack leaves the bait on the hook
the mermaids listen up: audible distortions and the deafening roar of "No comment,"
which the mermaids jot in their books
but even if the stowaways are thrown to the squids
the commodores can't keep a lid on the story; it's leaked
in the driftwood, in the rookery, in the dory in the belly of the catch;
the coda is, "It's trash"
it's sorrow dog's chew toy, and worse—
it's the skeleton ship's cargo, it's clamshelled desires and seventy brands of thirst
Water bottles everywhere, far, far too much to drink

after the deluge, garbage
garbage in Yangon and garbage in Chittagong
garbage in New Orleans
so much garbage, a map of the garbage,
the garbage as seen from the moon
"Every day all day, all day every day,"
says the garbage man hauling garbage
Freon garbage and mercury garbage and
maggot garbage and microwave garbage
birds' feet sinking in garbage
before the Army Corps slips out the back door,
they levee the city in garbage

do I bottom feed, love? do the mermaids scavenge?
the mermaids adore forgotten things, and my vision's aslant as a fluke's
but even a fisheries manager sometimes concedes a fine kettle of fish;
where the minnows hatch twisted as opera plots, and tadpoles pan for false teeth,
here, we plead guilty to the violence of holding our breath;
oh, Pliny the Elder, somebody duped you: a goby can't hold back an emperor's ship—
despite the little sucker's grip, the invaders arrive, the conquest betides,
the skeptics are skewered and pickled in brine, and the naive are hunted like dodos;
from here to the harbor, a view of the skyline, its cell blocks and fishbowls and kennels
romance a mammalian diving reflex that pushes us off the bridge of suspense,
its twinkling lights fist-sized; "Money ain't worth everything,"
says the man in the house by the coal ash pond on Needmore Avenue;
Alexandria's residents knew they were sinking, but the open-billed stork? not a clue;
astronauts washed up, gasping for air on the antique beaches of Mars

where the alewives pay in silver, the water-lords are known by their purse,
their wet nurse the toothless Chesapeake, its fangs yanked out by the seines
on the tails of spotter planes and hoovered into a freezer; the teaser, "a lifetime of health,"
the yo-ho-ho in the stealth dumping of fish oil into packaged cookies;
the Bush king, a rookie at snuffling truffles, packed up his duffles and
abandoned his rigs to the covert drove swarming the Bay of Pigs,
as the gumshoe fell from the other foot and landed on the head of menhaden,
a fish laden with liquid gold, sold by the ton for chicken shit;
it was Squanto who pitied the Pilgrims enough
to teach them to stuff a fish in the dirt with the corn,
the industrial feast of farm-bound beasts our mournful Thanksgiving
to a fish whose name means "mulch," the bay an emptied gulch;
Myles Standish, or Captain John Smith, could have walked like Jesus on water,
so thick were the "Fishe as no mans fortune hath ever possessed the like"—
the numbers of fish were so alarming, one wonders why they bothered with farming
but such are Pilgrims who seem to want hardship in order to thrive;
the Chesapeake was alive with oysters as thick as thighs and bass the size of women;
menhaden, its former filter and feed, no match for the speed of the factory catch,
were snatched up for soap and for rust-busting paint, and the starving bass ain't biting
now that there's nothing to bite; their breakfast was plucked
and trucked through the night hundreds of miles away
to feed bass who live behind bars

April 17, 2007: Following krill on the heels of the gulls, said to be souls of drowned sailors, a tiny minke whale, 5,000 pounds, 12 feet long, and, at one year old, a baby, enters the mouth of the Gowanus Canal, a Brooklyn waterway which, through the years, has hosted gristmills, tanneries, stone yards, coal yards, gas plants, cement works, paint factories, ink factories, soap factories, machine shops, sulfur plants, chemical works, and rafts of raw sewage. Lead, oil, mercury, cyanide, asbestos, VOCs, SVOCs, cholera, typhoid, typhus, and gonorrhea, the sludge at its bottom is dubbed "black mayonnaise." It is the day past the day that 32 people are shot and killed at Virginia Tech. The minke whale attracts onlookers hoping for better news. But the minke whale disappoints. She swims for two days. She splashes, she hits the dock, and she dies. Her pale underside is streaked with blood. She is known to the cops and the Coast Guard officials as NY 3673-07. But the onlookers name her Sludgie. In the days past her death, we will sew Sludgie pillows and crochet ourselves small Sludgie dolls. Thirty-four million years ago, four-legged creatures lost their hind limbs. Deer-like, no larger than cashmere sweaters, these were the ancestors of whales.

where wet meets dry under amplified sky,
raw in my hide at the lip of the lake, this suck-bone, Noachian skeleton,
I croon a small tune at the grebes and white pelicans, a spoiler on their bank
Down in the meadow in a little bitty pool, swam three little fishies and a mama fishie too
Kit Carson, dank with dead beaver, stampeded the groaning prairie grasses,
leading a party of addicts and asses over the South Pass
to this crack-den desert of needles and scablands where we bag the stream for a hit;
reclamation's some good shit: votes and the dope we call water,
be damned the sons and the daughters of the folks who were here before us;
in the baccarat lounge, the gangrened land's brand manager nods out
to the jingle's whitewashed chorus: *"Swim" said the mama fishie,*
"Swim if you can," and they swam and they swam all over the dam
the spawning upstream is paved these days, and over-policed like the border,
a tall order for the bottom dwellers, poor suckers, and the trout resigned to the hook,
fin-knotched and face-tagged and booked; still, it's better than an empty pot;
on bone-dry land in a concrete sloop, the mother of fishes hatches millions of songs,
escorting her miniscule riches through the gate to the lake in which they belong,
this dusty bowl's terminal spoonful of ancient inland ocean
while I, a rambling commotion, press on, in my rented kit and caboodle,
fossil-fueled, preachy, and punny until—bumpity-bump—dead bunny
dog dashing out on the Paiute road slurps the corpse up like a noodle

an extraordinary rendition of a shroud forms on shore, its vicious wanderlust calving
"These tourists want sun and beach," says the hotelier, his tan catastrophic
"If they don't have sand, they get angry"; Long John Silver's toxic box
brimming with carbon offset credits, the parrot spewing exhaust
a seashell full of amnesia, a seashell full of blood and guts
the craze in caution-tape bikinis, telecommuting for soldiers of fortune:
how a finger on the trigger in the Gulf of Oman can doodle on a napkin in Pismo Beach
a child asks for a glass of water, and sometimes the child is permitted to drink;
what the Salton Sea shares with the spring of Apollo: the oracular impulse in fish;
where beauty is an aerosol can disengorging a throat-stinging stand-in for aquamarine,
everyone taken to holster-bound thighs, to stockpiling shark fin soup;
below, Moby Dick stuffs her fat ass into a blip on the sonar,
the tear drop's worth of Britannia's oceans begrudged to marine protection
above, Filet-O-Fish sandwich, the glamour of sea legs and lunatic eights
a boy in the bathtub's "toy boat, toy boat" by the name of *American Triumph*

in a Florida lagoon, the deflated balloon of a reverie moister than Jacques Cousteau,
a Grecian urn creamed in a shipwreck, the ocean a den of intrigue littered with spy decoder rings
eyes the size of dinner plates, biologists blink at the immeasurable black
sorrow dog, blind Ganges dolphin, blinks her fallow eyes back
while polar bears, twinkle-toed, mince their retreat over the onion-skin ice,
corporate weathercocks take the pulse on the profit of making nice-nice
"It makes me feel lonely," says the islander clutching a one-way pass from the swallowed shore
the mermaids surf the crashing heat waves, the Gulag drips on the floor,
a hypodermic aftermath to the cryptozoological pool party, Loch Ness monster nuzzling junk;
at the bottom-captain's all-hands-on-deck, the crew goes kerplunk for the legend of swimming cunt,
casting and casting and casting about for the loophole in science's latest brute scoop:
when a fish is yanked from 3,000 feet under, it cries like a baby
as its gills hit the juice in this meth lab we know as the air

sorrow dog died, oh love of mine, sorrow dog died and is gone
we buried her where the fishermen hide from flat-footed women and hogs
we buried her under the water-sky where the bleeding fish bleed on the rod
we buried her by the water-rat reeds on the shores of the ditch they call "lake"
we buried her in the bottomlands, we buried her on the ache of an evening
where it's nicked by the night; happy dog's dead, my love, and gone,
happy dog's gone out of sight; may the cattail and pennywort and purslane
bend down, weave sorrow dog's soul a weed packet, and cast her out to float
amid the ducks and the snoring geese

on the heartbreak horizon at the go-for-broke well, sea slobs swarm from their deep-water shell,
shaped like sheens or slicks or gobs, or worse, tiny treats in a Tyvek purse
dispersed at the morning meeting, a unified mob pluming from the cracked skull of man,
a Pandora's box loosed, its black-butter grief uncanned on the razor clams and spring-tide scamps,
a tar-and-feather revamp of the marshland where the regulatory rubber stamps dock,
a lockdown on the laughing of gulls, their hardy-har-har gunked up tight;
it's night on the blood-dimmed gulf between ethics and murk,
it's a knife blade plunged 20,000 leagues deep into the heart of the bottom;
the feast upwells time and again, managers dab mouths with cut-and-paste plans,
the oceans are dragged from frying pan to fire, and the indignant shell-birds be damned;
the tanker will slam on the battering ram of the reef named for *Bounty's* captain
the tanker will dash and be turned to hash on the rocks off of Cornwall and Devon
the turn-turtle tanker will find a mangling in the strangling Straits of Magellan
and the rigs and the boats and the pipes will bring hell on the waters at Galveston,
Guanabara, Campeche, Port Sulphur, Karachi, Makushin and Skan,
Queensland, Port Arthur, Portsall, Stavanger, Genoa, and Bandar Abbas, Iran
and the seas will lose their living then, giving in to stony sleep

here lies the wreck of the *Dauntless*, here lies the wreck of the *Dawn*,
the wreck of the *Herald*, the wreck of *Eureka*, the wrecks of *Surprise* and *Relief*,
this is the wreck of *Halcyon*, the wreck of the *Lazy Days*,
here lies the wreck of *Harmony*, the wrecks of *Humanity* and *Hope*,
this is the wreck of *Independence*, the wreck of the *Fourth of July*,
here is the wreck of *Galilee*, the wreck of the *Golden Rule*,
the wreck of the *Far West*, the wreck of the *New World*, the wreck of the *Pioneer*,
here lies the wreck of *Fidelty*, of *Confidence* and *Liberty* and *Reliance*,
this is the wreck of *Yours Truly*, the wreck of *My Pride* and the *Pride of the Sea*,
here lies the wreck of the *Stranger*, here lies the wreck of *Home*
full fathom five, we sink and we dive, off the coast of California
if the murk and the crush and the rush of fear for the bite at our backs disarms us, love,
let us make like jewel squid at 5,000 feet,
one eye trained on the darkness, and the other bulging toward light

the mermaids sit in the yellow diner flummoxed by the waffles
they have heard there is no time like the present
but the present seems only palimpsest: a napkin stained with disastrous spills,
a view of the streets out the picture window through sheets of driving rain;
the waitress bores down wagging the check, an aerial map of nickles and dimes,
a ghostly grid of niggling debt atop a wobble-mouthed anamensis;
if the past and future are palindrome, think the mermaids,
this present is an incessant interruption

eh-oh seagull, eh-oh seal. here comes another grandiloquent entrance,
an onamonopoeic blow-the-man-down on the bottom's gaseous patience
the boring role of boring holes, a month at sea on a waste dump
as the stock market reels in its downtown berth, drunk as a pinafored ship's chimp
"There was no enforcement," says the Mineral Management Services drudge,
federal oversight falling apart for a pirate's sweet booty and a barrel of sludge
up against Davey Jones' locker, a session of "ultra-deep shelf play,"
a drilling more tempting than sex; it's a press gang drop-kicking pelicans' nests,
fugitive broods of boobies in masks, a speargun that shoots around corners
it's a turtle in a life vest turning and turning a widening gyre in the animal hospital kiddie pool
"It's like a Band-Aid to a gunshot wound to the heart," says the marine ornithologist
Captain Bligh got a poke in the eye, humping breadfruit for dominion's apologists
and died Vice Admiral of the Blue, a hue having less to do with the ocean than
the ink on the bill of lading for a cargo of imperial rot,
collapsitarians storming the melting buttery beneath the never-set blot
"We're milking this cow any way we can," says the acquisition geophysicist

the mermaids dream they are flying on a carpet of flying fish above a sequin and glitter sea
the mermaids are clean as can be; they smell of hot rock and of splashing
music wallows from the fiddler crab hollows, sperm whales and manatees chirp
dragonfish ignite their ravishing lights, the bamboo coral glows, the dark is usurped
there is softness (sargassum), complexity (mangrove), security (cordgrass), there's treasure,
measured in the oyster's magical itch and the pitch of the facets on the diamondback's shell;
on the swell of the endlessly creatured tide, loggerheads and leatherbacks pull for home
in the gloaming below, there is soup, and everyone is eating:
the tuna, the red drum, the chain cat shark, eating their fill, teeming at will, and spawning
the pelicans are yawning, the anchovies dancing, the river romancing the bay,
shipping scars and the names of things washed away in the unconcerned surf;
the mermaids have dreamed an incomparable future,
the present receding as in a painting thick with oils and hung on a wall,
a superb portrait of a ghost-ridden yawl, elaborately framed, behind glass;
in the bottled dawn, the mermaids wake, knowing
shake sea snails from their locks, recommence with their rowing

snowmen forging end-user permits, sweating like pigs in their top hats,
perform the exploding faucet trick, then saw the Marcellus Shale in two as if it's a lady in spangles,
uncontrolled discharge pooling about the bottom of their coal-button girths;
it's a regimen for a piddling planet based on enormous rates of leakage,
a filibuster drilled in the heart of the fractious debate between *ooh* and *aah*;
"It just hits a primal cord with people," sniffles the orphaned rabbit,
hopping away from the scene of the crime, a puddle of butter and crumbs;
"Suppose we change the subject," the March Hare interrupted, yawning.
"I'm getting tired of this. I vote the young lady tells us a story."
Once upon a time, there was a mermaid who pined for a pretty prince.
She scraped up a couple of clams and swam to a quack who laid her limbs,
which ended, not in feet, but in knives that gouged out the remnant scales on her ankles.
People, who favor such painful surrender, mistook the blades for wings
and immortalized her in stone and ink, a fish story worthy of Disney.

oh, this is a tale of the savorous seas and the port of a rummy town
where the mangoes drop atop your head and leave you a touch unsound
where the coin belongs to the dock merchant's purse
and to earn it, we all went aground:
the surfer with herpes, the castaway girl, the mutineer hiding from law and order
the diver who speared beautiful fish and spoke with a bubbling stutter
the cook who climbed coconut trees for the love of the landlubber's daughter
the Phoenician who crept from the cane fields to ponder death by water
we washed pots on shore by day for a nickel, dime, or quarter
we swam home to rusty moorings by the moonbow's improbable splendor
but some of us proved shorter
on a taste for brined breeze, the spinnaker's tantrums, the mainsail and mizzen's fervor
me, in my ardor for rock-solid wage and the slap of smart heel on paver,
shoved off in a miserable cage in the air, a crop-dusting helicopter
yes, I said goodbye to my port of call and my lice-bitten shipmates forever
now I wonder, by and by, if they live or have died as I stand in my street
beneath the dry mackerel sky by the concrete shells of foreclosure

give them a boardwalk, and people will walk on it—hello casino, hello paid parking,
looks like the whole huge ocean gets up, gets up and falls over, falls over again,
oh the body and its SPFs, its SPFs and its burn lines, its rolls of fat and its hairs,
Aeolian tug of the public toilets, the winos, the baby in sun bonnet stuff-faced with slobbery sand;
Patches the horse lived to dive from 40 feet high above Steel Pier into a little bucket,
"fuck it," thought Patches, and jumped; Donald Trump in a sharkskin suit
chews up the joint like it's salt water taffy, frenzied over ka-ching;
On the boardwalk in Atlantic City, we will walk in a dream
"You should have been there," my grandmother tells me.
She is 93 years old. She is on her nursing home death bed.
"I was in Atlantic City today. Everyone was there."
She names all the dead people. "Where were you?"
On the boardwalk in Atlantic City, life will be peaches and cream

I was raised to chase fury, my love, I was raised for the splashes
the rill had a thirst too big for its cup; it swallowed the house
from the bottom up and soaked me to my lashes; one might think it fun
to clap about in a mud-suck hole mistaken for rearing, but my father was steering—
he christened my mother, her bones for a hull, and left her a wreck in the storm drain;
sometimes you have to tell your tale plain—the rains came and washed away nothing

storm-bird and devil's-bird, spency and fieldfare, missel-thrush, thunderbird,
stilt stormy petrel, sea swallow, Tom-tailor, water-witch throng
their shrapnel-bite song the avian sound of the truth;
the harbor, aroused, uncurls its talons and shatters its soundproof booth,
revoking the street lamps and street signs and streets,
it beats its beats on its once-and-then drum, a rapture of repossession,
its rocketship wings casting umbrage upon this empire of things we call home,
the pixie-dust fling named ownership dissolving in the drink, a frothing like nuclear fission;
how a wall of water can mimick a bowl of whipped cream,
the dream of delicious sunsets a bunker in the dunes;
gutted like a fish, the frontage, a dish of spaghetti and spoons, broadcasts its paper-shredder tune:
the rift in the wake of the storm is the same as the rift in the path of the storm;
the mallet-headed harbor retreats, and the wind beats a path through the broken storm door
mermaids left gasping on the living room floor
plovers traipsing the grit-swept shore, pecking for traces of nest

gods and demons form a joint venture, milk Ursa Major for bile,
it's a life-jacket protocol for the doctrine of Limbo, flags up the ass of the Arctic;
past the bobtail squid and the cockatoo squid and the submersible holding the crackers,
past assonance, that headbanger's ball that is science's only real proof it exists—
say "bloody-belly comb jelly," say "glasshead grenadier," and science picks up the air guitar,
mouths the words to "Godzilla," that fad of false safety that swept Japan—
past the abyssal bite of the deep, to its acid-burn belly to pan Hades' gold;
Cerberus unlocks his three deep throats and howls up a heavy-metal racket
at the gigantism of the high-stakes grab at Davy Jones' gill-stuffed basket
in the now-you-see-it, now-you-don't tussle at the raw bar, our lust for Persephone gone pelagic,
International Sea Bed Authority the code name for a pocketful of sinkable hookers,
the key to the universe's hotel room an egg with an albatross inside

bored with the muddled floppings of Adam,
Lilith decamped and became her own madam
on the Red Seas' blushing shores, where she fucked the banshees,
then fucked them more, and for this she was sponged from the books;
lie low, oh mermaids, duck the hooks, hermitlike in your shell-less skins
loose lips on sinking ships whisper of sins, and you're fingered,
caught lingering with a fish mistaken for the soul of a lustrative saint;
Medusa in a hazmat suit, sopping up oil with her headful of mops,
finds lubed-up banshees mild slop compared to the Sound of Prince William
vomiting millions of gallons of crude; Poisedon, wagging his toxin beard,
trumpets woe to fastidious otters, woe to the herring and clams,
the *Exxon Valdez*, a corporate do-derring, is slapdashed with glue and nom de plume,
an *Oriental Nicety* sent back to sea where bristles and barbs sit in ambush

at the duty-free zone tiki bar, a man whose name means "sock on the jaw"
cuts arms deals in Esperanto, bemoans the global munitions glut—
MiGs worth less than cocktail nuts—orders a mai-tai pronto
in the lobster-bib afternoon, the clobbered lobster shells look like runes divining the old heave-ho
the bar maid counts her dubloons, the claws on her abacus fingers bedazzled by silicone tips
while in the burbling tank behind her, mermaids on leashes turn tricks

sea fairy, sea wizard, water-horse, sea-bean
picked clean on long conveyor belts and sorted by shape and size
how completely the meat is scooped from the shell; the world's fell
from the skies past the satellite that guides ships beyond reason
in the season of bone-sad tides; are they wise, the drowned,
who've found stillness while the rest of us flail? the Northern Passage,
the Arctic's third rail: fried fish and a polar bear rug,
our collective shrug as lethal as a blast pressure wound,
evidence forgotten as soon as it's archived; just the rats remember
that this spit of concrete between the highway and the street was once a wetland;
they scratch at the cracks here, hoping for water, and the daughters of the sinkholes,
the cloud-covered mermaids, sit down with soot in their fins

ask the humphorse spider crab, she knows no amount of eggs will do
they'll fall at you like a meteor storm and crack your back in two
they'll snatch the whirlpool sturgeon up and squeeze them for isinglass glue,
their frescoes flashing and blazing like fish scales, their gilded manuscripts, too,
depicting a nasty forecast coughed up by a fish with a stomach flu
the metropolis peeled like an onion and tumbled into the stew,
a bisque as fetid as a nursery rhyme with its salty collection-pond roux
fallen foul of the mermaids' appetite, who demurred and politely withdrew
from this banquet for thieves, donning floaties and flippers, and shuffling back to the blue

sorrow dog, forsaken by legs, sunk to the bottom of the hospital cage,
the medics squinting like the partially blind, a terror as taut as swim goggles;
it boggles the mind, the capaciousness of a dredger that would swallow a sorrow dog whole,
lover, let's make our way back to the ocean like turtles—we'll live for two million moons
the whales will surround us, and roll and swoon and hoot like it's Halloween
above us, engines and echo locators, the plate licked outrageously clean,
while down here, beyond the wet-knot tensions and the monofilament zeal
we'll stay whole-bellied, gentle, spongy together, dodging the casting reel
and conjuring humors and clamours to mend happy dog's leviathan heart

my love, you and I are by-the-wind sailors, sorted by right and wrong trades
we wobble like jelly, stinging each other in ballast-mouth, hard-swallow ways
our heads full of bite, transparently startled, we blaze like paper lamps
twist-notioned, drifting from point to point, beaching in free-float rants
we inflate ourselves like tutus, slinging the slang of the sunstroke marooned,
you the child of leagues-deep terrors, me the child of typhoons
there are many creatures in each of us, and each of them is hungry
we are hungry down here in the gigantic goo, and in prisms of sunlight,
we're hungry, too, in the midwater's bouyant unbounds
we are hungry, and sometimes we're fed
on the dazzle from top to bottom of the presence in which we live
when we go still and are quiet

shrimp boats storm the pelican rock, toeing their cocktail-sauce line
trawls like cuckoo clock pendulums, eleventh hour chimed
something goes bump in the inlet night, nearsighted sea lion with a lump on its skull
shies from the hull, barking into the dog-watch gloom
you dream greetings at slipside, mermaids in estrus, a channel betwixt warm and wet
I dream huddle in bull kelp, I dream holding my breath
or I dream vernal pool, I dream fairy shrimp, I dream quillworts on beach
you dream storm surge and shipwreck, you dream dashed on the reef
we spiral like barracudas, gnashing our jail-file teeth
at the bars on the brig in a sunken frigate christened the *Stop and Frisk*,
"Reasonableness is a Murky Standard" the motto of the ship;
in California's fog-brained dawn, a hangover branded by Boeing,
we brave, nonetheless, the destroyer's soft corpse, all of its bones showing
and we find it blooming with jewels:
señoritas amidst the barnacles soliciting rub-a-dub-dubs
anemones dandied in cerise and teal, the biggest draws in the club
starfish splayed like porn on the decks,
Garibaldis plotting unrest, dressed up as Molotov cocktails;
it's a riot, love, a candy store, the sea's delicious mess
why the ancients finished the undersides of things? they knew the gods would check

she's been here before the back beyond, this spider crab, this scavenger, *bandida* of the nets
before the gluing and the ungluing of the wild, wild west
before the butcher, baker, and candlestick maker washed up in their jalopy,
and disembarked their sloppy ark of pigs and sheep and donkeys,
who, having nothing more to eat, ate the island head to feet and burped a pile of gristle—
the monkey flower, bedstraw, lace pod, paintbrush swapped for European thistle;
before lift-off for a missile christened *Come When I Whistle II*
from the mani-pedi launch pad of this island nicknamed "fantasy" in the Kali Yuga dawn;
before Santa Ana winked her eye, dry as a Hollywood gimlet,
and peeled and twisted yachts like limes beached on the rims of inlets
before the island foxes rifled in the campers' trash for snacks
the spider crab, headlamps on, humped her half-a-million burdens through the wrack
they called her grotesque, a tangle of tubers and ulcers and spines swiping their bait at the pier,
but language has no reason or rhyme for a crab with 500,000 babies and the next shed near
like Gulliver who hoisted Lilliputians to his shoulders, she draped herself in barnacles,
and the barnacles took a ride with the air ferns and the moss dogs and the pink hearts side by side;
that was moons ago, when adornment had its purpose as disguise
and her shell was just another face to wear, then cast aside
an arm was just an arm then—she had ten; she could abide one being pried from her
by sailing men who played her like a lyre, plucking at her strings,
and in the do-re-me of branding, called her "California king";
it's a soup of stings, this ocean, it's a salt-broth Try Pots chowder
full of vampire birds and whiskered pelts and other starveling matter, but she's braved it
going soft each time, revising, one conclusion to the next, carrying on
until this last of last of molts, the final text; she's done with drafts
doors and windows bolted, she will stay, at last, inside
the lesson of the crab, my love? advance, and then be still; in time, everybody dies.

like the light keeper's keep—it isn't meant to be;
the lighthouse, for its part, will fall into the sea,
and the elephant seals will come back
they'll take to the lighthouse keeper's quarters, sliding inside through the cracks,
smelling profoundly of themselves and shitting fish on the floor
shedding a catastrophic mess in the bedrooms and parlor and store
and leaving the door ajar for the gulls
as January comes 'round once more

then we'll meet in the unsettled middle, love,
where the giant bells ring and the hatchetfish swing
and tentacled things fling a hula-skirt corkscrew ballet at the deep;
in the fracas below, we'll keep free of grenades but burst with illumination
my love, imagination squabbles like a cockatoo and, puppy-like, chases its tail
or, pluming, it opens in every direction, batting telescopical eyes and getting wise to the abyss;
this, dearest animal, is what we shall hunt for, our feelers fragile as float glass but long:
whalesong and tidbits of cooling light, delicious flashes of sense in this present tense of bursting shells,
a swell meal; chewing rough deals, bristlemouthed and real, but promising no further damage

in the woot-woot store-alarm crack-down dawn,
the mermaids shut mouths, and the mermaids get gone
from the clench at the bottom where they oftentimes hide;
the mermaids punt upwards, and flickering, rise;
for a moment, they wear the waves like a mask,
then the mermaids reach out, feel the walls of the air,
a tiny cell with room for a cot,
a swabber's lot, sorrow dog's last small gasp;
the mermaids clasp teeth on a note, muzzle the long low "ohhhh" of parting—
self from self, skin from fin, the sea below their human waists smarting
and smelling of blood; the mermaids rise,
with the glistening bivouac of sun in their eyes,
they squint and discern an outline;
it is the blueprint to a ship called *The World*,
a floating condominium of monstrous proportions,
a bobbing tin-pot in dusk's glinting distortions;
the mermaids look back, salt in their hair,
pinned for a moment on the dry page of fact:
it's been sadness from here to tadpole,
as the engines that make the giant yacht roll
churn on, such luxury a kind of redaction

I will cling to you like a mussel, my love, will you cling to me like a mussel?
We'll abide astride this dumb rock together, scarred and thin-shelled
and sometimes blue, but nevertheless hanging on;
mermaids, oh, sing your disavowed songs; bend your human limbs to their business:
with the pelicans and puffins and gulls and murres and elegant terns as your witness,
unloose the harbor seal lassoed by scratch, unloose his soft neck and his flippers
unloose his fat middle, his polka-dot cloak, unloose his wet eyes and his whiskers
spill the winds all over this trammel-mouth world, spill the seas up onto its beaches
I want the sun to come out, I want to sail us home, the mermaids sing,
I want the sun to come out, I want to sail us home

It's a planet made of ink on the arm of a sailor tricking in the head
where the slim wrist of morning is cuffed to the sink
to the bottom. The sea-dogs howl foul weather at the skies.
Whence the sea-dogs rise, there must be a kind of day,
for every dog has one; there must be some bed
where sleeping dogs lie and wake up without fleas.
When we've managed to pirate every molecule of the seas,
and replaced them with replicas rendered in plastic,
there, where the tail wags the sea-dog something fantastic,
will they witness our bathtub-ring finish, from space?
The face—if it's face—turns to the observable; a purl of blue,
a dusky scratch, a naked singularity cast in a font 10 million years gone;
still, the unmistakable signature of the presence of absence;
past the moon named Egg and the moon named Eggshell,
a crack in the well of the night, hydromantic and, perhaps,
just bright enough for you to find us
humble telescope,
find us

TRIBUTARIES

The Oxford English Dictionary; *The New York Times*; *The New York Post*; *AM New York*; *The New Yorker*; *Harper's Magazine*; *The Atlantic Monthly*; *U.S.A. Today*; *Popular Science*; *National Geographic*; *Sky*; *Time*; *Time for Kids*; *Mother Jones*; National Public Radio; The National Weather Service; The National Park Service; National Oceanic and Atmospheric Administration; National Aeronautics and Space Administration; United States Department of the Interior; United States Fish and Wildlife Service; The Marine Mammal Center; Waterkeeper Alliance; Ocean Conservancy; Nature Conservancy; Natural Resources Defense Council; National Audobon Society; Greenpeace; Agalita Marine Research Foundation; Monterey Bay Aquarium; Sierra Club; Georgia Sea Turtle Center; *The Woman's Dictionary of Symbols & Sacred Objects* and *The Woman's Encyclopedia of Myths & Secrets* by Barbara Walker; *The Herder Dictionary of Symbols*; *A Dictionary of Sea Terms* by Darcy Lever; *The Ocean Almanac* by Robert Hendrickson; *The Oxford Book of Sea Stories* edited by Tony Tanner; *The Encyclopedia of Seashells* by Gary Rosenberg; *What is a Shell?* by Lynn Scheu; *Eyewitness: Shell* by Alex Arthur; *Kingdom of the Seashell* by R. Tucker Abbott and Doris Townsend; *Shell Collecting: An Illustrated History* by S. Peter Dance; *Gift from the Sea* by Anne Morrow Lindbergh; *National Audobon Society Field Guide to North American Seashells*; *Oyster* and *The Duchess of Curiosities, The Life of Margaret, Duchess of Portland* by Rebecca Stott; *Natural History* by Pliny the Elder; *An Unnatural History of the Seas* by Callum Roberts; *Life Between the Tides: Marine Plants and Animals of the Northeast* by Les Watling, Jill Fegley, John Moring, and Susan K. White; *City at the Water's Edge: A Natural History of New York* by Betsy McCully; *The Other Islands of New York City: A History and Guide* by Sharon Seitz and Stuart Miller; *The Voyage of the Rose City* by John Moynihan; *The Odyssey* by Homer; *Four Fish* by Paul Greenberg; *Lobster* by Richard J. King; *Booty: Girl Pirates on the High Seas* by Sara Lorimer and Susan Synarski; *She Captains* by Joan Druett; *Horseshoe Crabs and Velvet Worms: The Story of the Animals and Plants That Time Has Left Behind* by Richard Fortey; *Monsters of the Deep* by Richard Ellis; *The Deep* by Claire Nouvian; *Reef* by Scubazoo; *Fire in the Turtle House: The Green Sea Turtle and the Fate of the Ocean* by Osha Gray Davidson; *Beautiful Swimmers* by William W. Warner; *Bottomfeeder: How to Eat Ethically in a World of Vanishing Seafood* by Taras Grescoe; *The World Without Us* by Alan Weisman; *Field Notes from a Catastrophe* by Elizabeth Kolbert; *Alice in Wonderland* by Lewis Carroll; "By the Beautiful Sea" by Harry Carroll and Harry R. Atteridge; "Sinking in the Lonesome Sea" by The Carter Family; "Three Little Fishies" by Saxie Dowell; "On the Boardwalk in Atlantic City" by Mack Gordon and Josef Myrow; various websites on shanties and sea songs; Bob Baron; Samuel Coleridge; Anne Sexton; T.S. Eliot; William Butler Yeats, Alfred Lord Tennyson and the mermaids.

ACKNOWLEDGMENTS

For the time and space to write this book, the author thanks The MacDowell Colony, Kimmel Harding Nelson Center for the Arts, Djerassi Resident Artists Program, Hedgebrook, Penny and Bob Baron, Howard Abramson and Ann Marie Spinelli. For publishing excerpts of this book, the author thanks Poets for Living Waters, *Kadar Koli, BoogCity*, Colgate Writers Conference, *Stone Canoe, Bomb*, *VINCENT*, and *The Laurel Review*. A portion of the author's proceeds goes to The Marine Mammal Center in Sausalito, California, for the protection, rescue, and rehabilitation of marine mammals.

Photo by Carolyn Monastra

Betsy Andrews is the author of *New Jersey* (University of Wisconsin Press, 2007), winner of the Brittingham Prize in Poetry.
Her chapbooks include *She-Devil* (Sardines Press, 2004), *In Trouble* (BoogCity Press, 2004), and *Supercollider*, a collaboration with the artist Peter Fox. She is the executive editor of *Saveur* magazine.